To: _____

From: _____

Poems
of
Love

Poems of Love

UNION
SQUARE
& CO.

NEW YORK

UNION SQUARE & CO.

NEW YORK

UNION SQUARE & CO. and the distinctive Union Square & Co. logo are registered trademarks of Sterling Publishing Co., Inc.

Union Square & Co., LLC, is a subsidiary of Sterling Publishing Co., Inc.

ISBN 978-1-4549-4706-6
ISBN 978-1-4549-4739-4 (e-book)

For information about custom editions, special sales, and premium purchases, please contact specialsales@unionsquareandco.com.

Printed in the United States

2 4 6 8 10 9 7 5 3

unionsquareandco.com

Cover art by Yehrin Tong
Cover design by Melissa Farris
Interior design by Rich Hazelton

Contents

Discreet Love

"Because mine eyes can never have their fill"—Dante 3

Sonnet XVIII—William Shakespeare 4

To Celia—Ben Jonson 5

On a Stolen Kiss—George Wither 6

The Dream—John Donne. 7

"When, dearest, I but think of thee"—Sir John Suckling 9

Love for Love—Richard Brinsley Sheridan. 10

"She was a Phantom of Delight"—William Wordsworth. . . . 11

I Never Could Love Till Now—Matthew Gregory Lewis . . . 13

Echoes—Thomas Moore. 14

"She walks in beauty, like the night"—

     George Gordon, Lord Byron. 15

Love's Philosophy—Percy Bysshe Shelley 16

The Tide of Love—Thomas Hood. 17

How Many Times—Thomas Lovell Beddoes 18

Vivien's Song—Alfred, Lord Tennyson 19

Invitation to Love—Paul Laurence Dunbar 20

Passionate Love

Song (Mediocrity in Love Rejected)—Thomas Carew 23

To His Coy Mistress—Andrew Marvell 24

A Love-Lesson—Leigh Hunt 26

The Kiss—Samuel Taylor Coleridge 27

Regret—Charlotte Brontë 29

Remembrance—Emily Brontë 31

Sonnet XLIII (from *Sonnets from the Portuguese*)—
      Elizabeth Barrett Browning 33

Mid-Rapture—Dante Gabriel Rossetti 34

I Loved You First (from "Monna Innominata")—
      Christina Rossetti 35

Wild nights! Wild nights!—Emily Dickinson 36

Madonna Mia—Algernon Charles Swinburne 37

To a Loved One—Sappho 40

Fools for Love

The Faithful Lover—Sir Thomas Wyatt 43

A Red, Red Rose—Robert Burns 44

The Silent Lover—Sir Walter Raleigh 45

To Anthea, Who May Command Him Anything—
      Robert Herrick 47

A Song to Amoret—Henry Vaughan 49

Sonnet (To Fanny)—John Keats 51

"Love me or not, love her I must or die"—
      Thomas Campion 52

Annabel Lee—Edgar Allan Poe 53

Never Give All the Heart—William Butler Yeats 55

Discreet Love

"Because mine eyes can never have their fill"

Dante

Because mine eyes can never have their fill
Of looking at my lady's lovely face,
    I will so fix my gaze
That I may become blessed, beholding her
Even as an angel, up at his great height
Standing amid the light,
    Becometh blessed by only seeing God:—
So, though I be a simple earthly wight,
Yet none the less I might,
    Beholding her who is my heart's dear load,
    Be blessed, and in the spirit soar abroad.
Such power abideth in that gracious one;
Albeit felt of none
    Save of him who, desiring, honours her.

Sonnet XVIII

William Shakespeare

Shall I compare thee to a summer's day?
Thou art more lovely and more temperate:
Rough winds do shake the darling buds of May,
And summer's lease hath all too short a date:
Sometime too hot the eye of heaven shines,
And often is his gold complexion dimm'd;
And every fair from fair sometime declines,
By chance or nature's changing course untrimm'd;
But thy eternal summer shall not fade
Nor lose possession of that fair thou ow'st;
Nor shall death brag thou wander'st in his shade,
When in eternal lines to time thou grow'st;
    So long as men can breathe or eyes can see,
    So long lives this, and this gives life to thee.

To Celia

Ben Jonson

Drink to me only with thine eyes,
    And I will pledge with mine;
Or leave a kiss but in the cup,
    And I'll not look for wine.
The thirst, that from the soul doth rise,
    Doth ask a drink divine:
But might I of Jove's nectar sup,
    I would not change for thine.

I sent thee late a rosy wreath,
    Not so much honouring thee,
As giving it a hope, that there
    It could not wither'd be.
But thou thereon didst only breathe,
    And sent'st it back to me:
Since when it grows, and smells, I swear,
    Not of itself, but thee.

On a Stolen Kiss

George Wither

Now gentle sleep hath closed up those eyes
Which, waking, kept my boldest thoughts in awe;
And free access unto that sweet lip lies,
From whence I long the rosy breath to draw.
Methinks no wrong it were if I should steal
From those two melting rubies one poor kiss:
None sees the theft that would the theft reveal,
Nor rob I her of aught what she can miss;
Nay, should I twenty kisses take away
There would be little sign I would do so.
Why then should I this robbery delay?
O, she may wake, and therewith angry grow!
Well, if she do, I'll back restore that one,
And twenty hundred thousand more for loan.

The Dream

John Donne

Dear Love, for nothing less than thee
Would I have broke this happy dream;
    It was a theme
For reason, much too strong for phantasy,
Therefore thou waked'st me wisely; yet
My dream thou brok'st not, but continued'st it:
Thou art so true, that thoughts of thee suffice
To make dreams truths, and fables histories;
Enter these arms, for since thou thought'st it best
Not to dream all my dream, let's act the rest.

As lightning or a taper's light,
Thine eyes, and not thy noise waked me;
    Yet I thought thee
(For thou lov'st truth) an angel at first sight;
But when I saw thou saw'st my heart,
And knew'st my thoughts beyond an angel's art,
When thou knew'st what I dreamt, then thou knew'st
    when
Excess of joy would wake me, and cam'st then;
I must confess, it could not choose but be
Profane to think thee any thing but thee.

Coming and staying showed thee thee;
But rising makes me doubt that now
    Thou art not thou.

That Love is weak, where fear's as strong as he;
'Tis not all spirit, pure and brave,
If mixture it of fear, shame, honor, have.
Perchance as torches, which must ready be,
Men light and put out, so thou deal'st with me,
Thou cam'st to kindle, goest to come: then I
Will dream that hope again, but else would die.

"When, dearest, I but think of thee"

Sir John Suckling

When, dearest, I but think of thee,
Methinks all things that lovely be
 Are present, and my soul delighted:
For beauties that from worth arise
Are like the grace of deities,
 Still present thus, though unsighted.

Thus while I sit and sigh the day
With all his borrowed lights away,
 Till's nights black wings do overtake me,
Thinking on thee, thy beauties then,
As sudden lights do sleepy men,
 So they by their bright rays awake me.

Thus absence dies, and dying proves
No absence can subsist with loves
 That do partake of perfection:
Since in the darkest night they may
By love's quick motion find a way
 To see each other by reflection.

The waving sea can with each flood
Bathe some high promont that hath stood
 Far from the main up in the river:
O think not then but love can do
As much! For that's an ocean too,
 Which flows not every day, but ever!

Love for Love

Richard Brinsley Sheridan

I ne'er could any lustre see
In eyes that would not look on me;
I ne'er saw nectar on a lip
But where mine own did hope to sip.
Has the maid who seeks my heart
Cheeks of rose, untouched by art?
I will own the color true
When yielding blushes aid their hue.

Is her hand so soft and pure?
I must press it to be sure;
Nor can I be certain then,
Till it, grateful, press again.
Must I, with attentive eye,
Watch her heaving bosom sigh?
I will do so when I see
That heaving bosom sigh for me.

"She was a Phantom of Delight"

William Wordsworth

She was a Phantom of delight
When first she gleamed upon my sight;
A lovely Apparition, sent
To be a moment's ornament;
Her eyes as stars of Twilight fair;
Like Twilight's, too, her dusky hair;
But all things else about her drawn
From May-time and the cheerful Dawn;
A dancing Shape, an Image gay,
To haunt, to startle, and waylay.

I saw her upon nearer view,
A Spirit, yet a Woman too!
Her household motions light and free,
And steps of virgin liberty;
A countenance in which did meet
Sweet records, promises as sweet;
A Creature, not too bright or good
For human nature's daily food;
For transient sorrows, simple wiles,
Praise, blame, love, kisses, tears,
    and smiles.

And now I see with eye serene
The very pulse of the machine;
A perfect Woman, nobly planned,
To warn, to comfort, and command;
And yet a Spirit still, and bright
With something of an angel light.

I Never Could Love Till Now

Matthew Gregory Lewis

When I gaze on a beautiful face
    Or a form which my fancy approved,
I was pleased with its sweetness and grace,
    And falsely believed that I loved.
But my heart, though I strove to deceive,
    The imposture it would not allow;
I could look, I could like, I could leave,
    But I could never love—till now.

Yet though I from others could rove,
    Now harbor no doubt of my truth,
Those flames were not lighted by love,
    They were kindled by folly and youth.
But no longer of reason bereft.
    On your hand, that pure altar, I vow,
Though I have looked, and I've liked, and have
        left—
    That I have never loved—till now.

Echoes

Thomas Moore

How sweet the answer Echo makes
    To Music at night,
When, roused by lute or horn, she wakes,
And far away o'er lawns and lakes
    Goes answering light!

Yet Love hath echoes truer far,
    And far more sweet
Than e'er, beneath the moonlight's star,
Of horn, or lute, or soft guitar,
    The songs repeat.

'Tis when the sigh,—in youth sincere,
    And only then,—
The sigh that's breathed for one to hear,
Is by that one, that only dear,
    Breathed back again.

"She walks in beauty like the night"

George Gordon, Lord Byron

She walks in beauty, like the night
    Of cloudless climes and starry skies;
And all that's best of dark and bright
    Meet in her aspect and her eyes:
Thus mellow'd to that tender light
    Which heaven to gaudy day denies.

One shade the more, one ray the less,
    Had half impair'd the nameless grace
Which waves in every raven tress,
    Or softly lightens o'er her face;
Where thoughts serenely sweet express
    How pure, how dear their dwelling-place.

And on that cheek, and o'er that brow,
    So soft, so calm, yet eloquent,
The smiles that win, the tints that glow,
    But tell of days in goodness spent,
A mind at peace with all below,
    A heart whose love is innocent!

Love's Philosophy

Percy Bysshe Shelley

I

The fountains mingle with the river
    And the rivers with the Ocean,
The winds of Heaven mix for ever
    With a sweet emotion;
Nothing in the world is single;
    All things by a law divine
In one spirit meet and mingle.
    Why not I with thine?—

II

See the mountains kiss high Heaven
    And the waves clasp one another;
No sister-flower would be forgiven
    If it disdained its brother;
And the sunlight clasps the earth
    And the moonbeams kiss the sea:
What is all this sweet work worth—
    If thou kiss not me?—

The Tide of Love

Thomas Hood

Still glides the gentle streamlet on,
With shifting current new and strange;
The water that is here is gone,—
But those green shadows never change.
Serene, or ruffled by the storm,
On present waves as on the past,
The mirrored grove retains its form,
The selfsame trees their semblance cast.
The hue each fleeting globule wears,
That drop bequeaths it to the next:
One picture still the surface bears,
To illustrate the murmured text.
So, love, however time may flow,
Fresh hours pursuing those that flee,
One constant image still shall show
My tide of life is true to thee.

How Many Times

Thomas Lovell Beddoes

How many times do I love thee, dear?
    Tell me how many thoughts there be
        In the atmosphere
        Of a new-fall'n year,
Whose white and sable hours appear
    The latest flake of Eternity:
So many times do I love thee, dear.

How many times do I love, again?
    Tell me how many beads there are
        In a silver chain
        Of the evening rain,
Unravelled from the tumbling main,
    And threading the eye of a yellow star:
So many times do I love, again.

Vivien's Song

Alfred, Lord Tennyson

In Love, if Love be Love, if Love be ours,
Faith and unfaith can ne'er be equal powers;
Unfaith in aught is want of faith in all.

It is the little rift within the lute
That, by and by, will make the music mute,
And, ever widening, slowly silence all:

The little rift within the lover's lute,
Or little pitted speck in garnered fruit,
That, rotting inward, slowly moulders all.

It is not worth the keeping: let it go!
But shall it? answer, darling, answer No!
And trust me not at all, or all in all.

Invitation to Love

Paul Laurence Dunbar

Come when the nights are bright with stars
Or come when the moon is mellow;
Come when the sun his golden bars
Drops on the hay-field yellow.
Come in the twilight soft and gray,
Come in the night or come in the day,
Come, O love, whene'er you may,
And you are welcome, welcome.

You are sweet, O Love, dear Love,
You are soft as the nesting dove.
Come to my heart and bring it to rest
As the bird flies home to its welcome nest.

Come when my heart is full of grief
Or when my heart is merry;
Come with the falling of the leaf
Or with the redd'ning cherry.
Come when the year's first blossom blows,
Come when the summer gleams and glows,
Come with the winter's drifting snows,
And you are welcome, welcome.

Passionate Love

Song

Thomas Carew

Give me more love, or more disdain:
    The torrid, or the frozen zone
Bring equal ease unto my pain;
    The temperate afford me none:
Either extreme of love or hate,
Is sweeter than a calm estate.

Give me a storm; if it be love,
    Like Danaë in that golden shower,
I swim in pleasure; if it prove
    Disdain, that torrent will devour
My vulture-hopes; and he's possessed
Of heaven, that's but from hell released.

The crown my joys, or cure my pain:
Give me more love, or more disdain.

To His Coy Mistress

Andrew Marvell

Had we but world enough and time,
This coyness, lady, were no crime.
We would sit down and think which way
To walk, and pass our long love's day.
Thou by the Indian Ganges' side
Shouldst rubies find: I by the tide
Of Humber would complain. I would
Love you ten years before the flood,
And you should, if you please, refuse
Till the conversion of the Jews;
My vegetable love should grow
Vaster than empires and more slow;
An hundred years should go to praise
Thine eyes, and on thy forehead gaze;
Two hundred to adore each breast,
But thirty thousand to the rest;
An age at least to every part,
And the last age should show your heart.
For, lady, you deserve this state,
Nor would I love at lower rate.

But at my back I always hear
Time's wingèd chariot hurrying near,
And yonder all before us lie
Deserts of vast eternity.

Thy beauty shall no more be found,
Nor in thy marble vault shall sound
My echoing song: then worms shall try
That long-preserved virginity,
And your quaint honour turn to dust,
And into ashes all my lust:
The grave's a fine and private place,
But none, I think, do there embrace.

Now, therefore, while the youthful hue
Sits on thy skin like morning dew,
And while thy willing soul transpires
At every pore with instant fires,
Now, let us sport us while we may,
And now, like amorous birds of prey
Rather at once our time devour,
Than languish in his slow-chaped power.
Let us roll all our strength and all
Our sweetness up into one ball,
And tear our pleasures with rough strife,
Thorough the iron gates of life;
Thus, though we cannot make our sun
Stand still, yet we will make him run.

A Love-Lesson
(FROM THE FRENCH OF CLÉMENT MAROT)

Leigh Hunt

A sweet "No, no!"—with a sweet smile beneath,—
Becomes an honest girl; I'd have you learn it.
As for plain "Yes!" —it may be said, i' faith,
Too plainly, and too oft: pray, well discern it.

Not that I'd have my pleasure incomplete,
Or lose the kiss for which my lips beset you;
But that in suffering me to take it, sweet,
I'd have you say, "No, no! I will not let you!"

The Kiss

Samuel Taylor Coleridge

One kiss, dear maid! I said, and sighed:
Your scorn the little boon denied.
Ah! why refuse the blameless bliss?
Can danger lurk within a kiss?

Yon viewless wanderer of the vale,
The spirit of the western gale,
At morning's break, at evening's close,
Inhales the sweetness of the rose,
And hovers o'er the uninjured bloom,
Sighing back the soft perfume;
Vigor to the zephyr's wing
Her nectar-breathing kisses fling;
And he the glitter of the dew
Scatters on the rose's hue.
Bashful, lo! she bends her head,
And darts a blush of deeper red.

Too well those lovely lips disclose
The triumphs of the opening rose:
O fair! O graceful! bid them prove
As passive to the breath of love.
In tender accents, faint and low,
Well pleased, I hear the whispered "No!"
The whispered "No!"—how little meant!
Sweet falsehood that endears consent!

For on those lovely lips the while
Dawns the soft relenting smile,
And tempts with feigned dissuasion coy
The gentle violence of joy.

Regret

Charlotte Brontë

Long ago I wished to leave
    "The house where I was born";
Long ago I used to grieve,
    My home seemed so forlorn.
In other years, its silent rooms
    Were filled with haunting fears;
Now their very memory comes
    O'ercharged with tender tears.

Life and marriage I have known,
    Things once deemed so bright;
Now how utterly is flown
    Every ray of light!
Mid the unknown sea of life
    I no blest isle have found;
At last, through all its wild waves strife,
    My bark is homeward bound.

Farewell, dark and rolling deep!
    Farewell, foreign shore!
Open, in unclouded sweep,
    Thou glorious realm before!
Yet, though I had safely pass'd
    That weary, vexed main,
One loved voice, through surge and blast,
    Could call me back again.

Though the soul's bright morning rose
    O'er Paradise for me,
William! even from Heaven's repose
    I'd turn, invoked by thee!
Storm nor surge should e'er arrest
    My soul, exulting then:
All my heaven was once thy breast,
    Would it were mine again!

Remembrance

Emily Brontë

Cold in the earth—and the deep snow piled above thee,
Far, far, removed, cold in the dreary grave!
Have I forgot, my only Love, to love thee,
Severed at last by Time's all-severing wave?

Now, when alone, do my thoughts no longer hover
Over the mountains, on that northern shore,
Resting their wings where heath and fern-leaves cover
Thy noble heart for ever, ever more?

Cold in the earth—and fifteen wild Decembers,
From those brown hills, have melted into spring:
Faithful, indeed, is the spirit that remembers
After such years of change and suffering!

Sweet Love of youth, forgive, if I forget thee,
While the world's tide is bearing me along;
Other desires and other hopes beset me,
Hopes which obscure, but cannot do thee wrong!

No later light has lightened up my heaven,
No second morn has ever shone for me;
All my life's bliss from thy dear life was given,
All my life's bliss is in the grave with thee.

But, when the days of golden dreams had perished,
And even Despair was powerless to destroy;
Then did I learn how existence could be cherished,
Strengthened, and fed without the aid of joy.

Then did I check the tears of useless passion—
Weaned my young soul from yearning after thine;
Sternly denied its burning wish to hasten
Down to that tomb already more than mine.

And, even yet, I dare not let it languish,
Dare not indulge in memory's rapturous pain;
Once drinking deep of that divinest anguish,
How could I seek the empty world again?

Sonnet XLIII
(from *Sonnets from the Portuguese*)

Elizabeth Barrett Browning

How do I love thee? Let me count the ways.
I love thee to the depth and breadth and height
My soul can reach, when feeling out of sight
For the ends of Being and ideal Grace.
I love thee to the level of everyday's
Most quiet need, by sun and candle-light.
I love thee freely, as men strive for Right;
I love thee purely, as they turn from Praise.
I love thee with the passion put to use
In my old griefs, and with my childhood's faith.
I love thee with a love I seemed to lose
With my lost saints,—I love thee with the breath,
Smiles, tears, of all my life!—and, if God choose,
I shall but love thee better after death.

Mid-Rapture

Dante Gabriel Rossetti

Thou lovely and beloved, thou my love;
    Whose kiss seems still the first; whose summoning
        eyes,
    Even now, as for our love-world's new sunrise,
Shed very dawn; whose voice, attuned above
All modulation of the deep-bowered dove,
    Is like a hand laid softly on the soul;
    Whose hand is like a sweet voice to control
Those worn tired brows it hath the keeping of:—

What word can answer to thy word,—what gaze
    To thine, which now absorbs within its sphere
    My worshipping face, till I am mirrored there
Light-circled in a heaven of deep-drawn rays?
    What clasp, what kiss mine inmost heart can prove,
    O lovely and beloved, O my love?

I Loved You First
(from "Monna Innominata")

Christina Rossetti

I loved you first: but afterwards your love,
    Outsoaring mine, sang such a loftier song
As drowned the friendly cooings of my dove.
    Which owes the other most? My love was long,
    And yours one moment seemed to wax more strong;
I loved and guessed at you, you construed me
And loved me for what might or might not be—
    Nay, weights and measures do us both a wrong.
For verily love knows not "mine" or "thine";
    With separate "I" and "thou" free love has done,
      For one is both and both are one in love:
Rich love knows nought of "thine that is not mine";
      Both have the strength and both the length
        thereof,
    Both of us, of the love which makes us one.

"Wild nights! Wild nights!"

Emily Dickinson

Wild nights! Wild nights!
Were I with thee,
Wild nights should be
Our luxury!

Futile the winds
To a heart in port,—
Done with the compass,
Done with the chart.

Rowing in Eden!
Ah! the sea!
Might I but moor
To-night in thee!

Madonna Mia

Algernon Charles Swinburne

Under green apple boughs
That never a storm will rouse,
My lady hath her house
    Between two bowers;
In either of the twain
Red roses full of rain;
She hath for bondwomen
    All kind of flowers.

She hath no handmaid fair
To draw her curled gold hair
Through rings of gold that bear
    Her whole hair's weight;
She hath no maids to stand
Gold-clothed on either hand;
In all that great green land
    None is so great.

She hath no more to wear
But one white hood of vair
Drawn over eyes and hair,
    Wrought with strange gold,
Made for some great queen's head,
Some fair great queen since dead;
And one strait gown of red
    Against the cold.

Beneath her eyelids deep
Love lying seems asleep,
Love, swift to wake, to weep,
    To laugh, to gaze;
Her breasts are like white birds,
All her gracious words
As water-grass to herds
    In the June-days.

To her all dews that fall
And rains are musical;
Her flowers are few from all,
    Her joys from these;
In the deep-feathered firs
Their gift of joy is hers,
In the least breath that sirs
    Across the trees.

She grows with greenest leaves,
Ripens with reddest sheaves,
Forgets, remember, grieves,
    And is not sad;
The quiet lands and skies
Leave light upon her eyes;
None knows her, weak or wise,
    Or tired or glad.

None knows, none understands,
What flowers are her hands;
Though you should search all lands
    Wherein time grows,

What snows are like her feet,
Though his eyes burn with heat
Though grazing on my sweet,—
     Yet no man knows.

Only this thing is said;
That white and gold and red,
God's three chief words, man's bread
     And oil and wine,
Were given her for dowers,
And kingdoms of all hours,
And grace of goodly flowers
     And various vine.

This is my lady's praise:
God after many days
Wrought in her unknown ways,
     In sunset lands;
This is my lady's birth;
God gave her right and mirth.
And laid his whole sweet earth
     Between her hands.

Under deep apple boughs
My lady hath her house;
She wears upon her brows
     The flower thereof;
All saying but what God saith
To her is as vain breath;
She is more strong than death,
     Being strong as love.

To a Loved One

Sappho

Translated by Ambrose Phillips

Bless'd as the immortal gods is he,
The youth who fondly sits by thee,
And hears and sees thee all the while
Softly speak and sweetly smile.

'Twas this depriv'd my soul of rest,
And rais'd such tumults in my breast;
For while I gaz'd, in transport toss'd,
My breath was gone, my voice was lost:

My bosom glow'd; the subtle flame
Ran quick through all my vital frame;
O'er my dim eyes a darkness hung;
My ears with hollow murmurs rung.

In dewy damps my limbs were chill'd;
My blood with gentle horror thrill'd;
My feeble pulse forgot to play;
I fainted, sank, and died away.

Dare I well give, I say, my heart to year.

Fools for Love

The Faithful Lover

GIVETH TO HIS MISTRESS HIS HEART
AS HIS BEST FRIEND AND ONLY TREASURE

Sir Thomas Wyatt

To seek each where man doth live,
The sea, the land, the rock, the clive,
France, Spain, and Inde, and every where;
Is none a greater gift to give,
Less set by oft, and is so lief and dear,
Dare I well say, than that I give to year.

 I cannot give broaches nor rings,
These goldsmith work, and goodly things,
Pierrie, nor pearl, orient and clear;
But for all that can no man bring
Lieffer jewel unto his lady dear,
Dare I well say, than that I give to year.

 Nor I seek not to fetch it far;
Worse is it not tho' it be narr,
And as it is, it doth appear
Uncounterfeit mistrust to bar.
It is both whole, and pure, withouten peer,
Dare I will say, the gift I give to year.

 To thee therefore the same retain;
The like of thee to have again
France would I give, if mine it were.
Is none alive in whom doth reign
Lesser disdain; freely therefore lo! here
Dare I well give, I say, my heart to year.

A Red, Red Rose

Robert Burns

O, my luve's like a red, red rose,
    That's newly sprung in June:
O, my luve's like a melodie
    That's sweetly play'd in tune.

As fair art thou, my bonnie lass,
    So deep in love am I:
And I will love thee still, my dear,
    Till a' the seas gang dry.

Till a' the seas gang dry, my dear,
    And the rocks melt wi' the sun:
I will luve thee still, my dear,
    While the sands of life shall run.

And fare thee weel, my only love!
    And fare thee weel a while!
And I will come again, my luve,
    Tho' it were ten thousand mile.

The Silent Lover

Sir Walter Raleigh

Wrong not, sweet mistress of my heart,
    The merit of true passion,
With thinking that he feels no smart
    Who sues for no compassion.

Since if my plaints were not t' approve
    The conquest of thy beauty,
It comes not from defect of love,
    But fear t' exceed my duty.

For, knowing that I sue to serve
    A saint of such perfection
As all desire but none deserve
    A place in her affection,

I rather choose to want relief
    Than venture the revealing:—
Where glory recommends the grief,
    Despair disdains the healing.

Thus those desires that boil so high
    In any mortal lover,
When reason cannot make them die
    Discretion them must cover.

Yet when discretion doth bereave
    The plaints that I should utter,
Then your discretion may perceive
    That silence is a suitor.

Silence in love bewrays more woe
    Than words, though ne'er so witty:
A beggar that is dumb, you know,
    May challenge double pity.

Then wrong not, dearest to my heart,
    My love, for secret passion:
He smarteth most that hides his smart,
    And sues for no compassion.

To Anthea, Who May Command Him Anything

Robert Herrick

Bid me to live, and I will live
    Thy Protestant to be;
Or bid me love, and I will give
    A loving heart to thee.

A heart as soft, a heart as kind,
    A heart as sound and free
As in the whole world thou canst find.
    That heart I'll give to thee.

Bid that heart stay, and it will stay
    To honor thy decree;
Or bid it languish quite away,
    And 't shall do so for thee.

Bid me to weep, and I will weep,
    While I have eyes to see;
And having none, yet I will keep
    A heart to weep for thee.

Bid me despair, and I'll despair,
    Under that cypress tree;
Or bid me die, and I will dare
    E'en death, to die for thee.

Thou art my life, my love, my heart,
    The very eyes of me;
And hast command of every part,
    To live and die for thee.

A Song to Amoret

Henry Vaughan

If I were dead, and, in my place,
　Some fresher youth designed
To warm thee, with new fires; and grace
　Those arms I left behind:

Were he as faithful as the Sun,
　That's wedded to the Sphere;
His blood as chaste and temperate run,
　As April's mildest tear;

Or were he rich; and, with his heap
　And spacious share of earth,
Could make divine affection cheap,
　And court his golden birth;

For all these arts, I'd not believe
　(No! though he should be thine!),
The mighty Amorist could give
　So rich a heart as mine!

Fortune and beauty thou might'st find,
　And greater men than I;
But my true resolvèd mind
　They never shall come nigh.

For I not for an hour did love,
  Or for a day desire,
But with my soul had from above
  This endless holy fire.

Sonnet

TO FANNY

John Keats

I cry your mercy—pity—love!—aye, love!
    Merciful love that tantalizes not,
One-thoughted, never-wandering, guileless love,
    Unmask'd, and being seen—without a blot!
O! let me have thee whole,—all—all—be mine!
    That shape, that fairness, that sweet minor zest
Of love, your kiss,—those hands, those eyes divine,
    That warm, white, lucent, million-pleasured
        breast,—
Yourself—your soul—in pity give me all,
Withhold no atom's atom or I die,
Or living on perhaps, your wretched thrall,
    Forget, in the mist of idle misery,
Life's purposes,—the palate of my mind
Losing its gust, and my ambition blind!

"Love me or not,
love her I must or die"

Thomas Campion

Love me or not, love her I must or die;
Leave her or not, follow her needs must I.
O that her grace would my wished comforts give!
How rich in her, how happy should I live!
All my desire, all my delight should be
Her to enjoy, her to unite to me;
Envy should cease, her would I love alone:
Who loves by looks, is seldom true to one.
Could I enchant, and that it lawful were,
Her would I charm softly that none should hear;
But love enforced rarely yields firm content:
So would I love that neither should repent.

Annabel Lee

Edgar Allan Poe

It was many and many a year ago,
    In a kingdom by the sea,
That a maiden there lived whom you may know
    By the name of Annabel Lee;—
And this maiden she lived with no other thought
    Than to love and be loved by me.

I was a child and *she* was a child,
    In this kingdom by the sea;
But we loved with a love that was more than love—
    I and my Annabel Lee—
With a love that the wingéd seraphs in Heaven
    Coveted her and me.

And this was the reason that, long ago,
    In this kingdom by the sea,
A wind blew out of a cloud, chilling
    My beautiful Annabel Lee;
So that her high-born kinsmen came
    And bore her away from me,
To shut her up in a sepulchre,
    In this kingdom by the sea.

The angels, not half so happy in Heaven,
    Went envying her and me—
Yes!—that was the reason (as all men know,
    In this kingdom by the sea)

That the wind came out of the cloud by night,
	Chilling and killing my Annabel Lee.

But our love it was stronger by far than the love
	Of those who were older than we—
Of many far wiser than we—
	And neither the angels in Heaven above,
Nor the demons down under the sea,
	Can ever dissever my soul from the soul
Of the beautiful Annabel Lee:—

For the moon never beams, without bringing me dreams
	Of the beautiful Annabel Lee;
And the stars never rise, but I feel the bright eyes
	Of the beautiful Annabel Lee:—
And so, all the night-tide, I lie down by the side
	Of my darling—my darling—my life and my bride,
	In her sepulchre there by the sea—
	In her tomb by the sounding sea.

Never Give All the Heart

William Butler Yeats

Never give all the heart, for love
Will hardly seem worth thinking of
To passionate women if it seem
Certain, and they never dream
That it fades out from kiss to kiss;
For everything that's lovely is
But a brief dreamy kind delight.
O never give the heart outright,
For they, for all smooth lips can say,
Have given their hearts up to the play
And who could play it well enough
If deaf and dumb and blind with love?
He that made this knows all the cost,
For he gave all his heart and lost.

Signature Select Classics

Elegantly Designed Booklets of Poetry and Prose

This book is part of Union Square & Co.'s Signature Select Classics chapbook series. Each booklet features distinguished poetry and prose by the world's greatest poets and writers in an elegantly designed and printed chapbook binding. Compact and portable, they fit comfortably in the hand and can be carried conveniently anywhere. These books are essential reading for lovers of classic literature and collectible editions in their own right. They make perfect keepsakes to own and to share with others.